STEAM AT WORK

STEAM AT WORK
Preserved Industrial Locomotives

Fred Kerr

PEN & SWORD
TRANSPORT

First published in Great Britain in 2017 by
Pen & Sword Transport
An imprint of
Pen & Sword Books Ltd
47 Church Street
Barnsley
South Yorkshire
S70 2AS

ISBN 978 1 47389 657 4

A CIP catalogue record for this book is
available from the British Library.

Typeset in 11pt Minion by Mac Style Ltd, Bridlington, East Yorkshire
Printed and bound in India by Replika Press Pvt Ltd

Pen & Sword Books Ltd incorporates the imprints of Pen & Sword Archaeology, Atlas, Aviation, Battleground,
Discovery, Family History, History, Maritime, Military, Naval, Politics, Railways, Select, Transport, True
Crime, and Fiction, Frontline Books, Leo Cooper, Praetorian Press, Seaforth Publishing and Wharncliffe.

For a complete list of Pen & Sword titles please contact
PEN & SWORD BOOKS LIMITED
47 Church Street, Barnsley, South Yorkshire, S70 2AS, England
E-mail: enquiries@pen-and-sword.co.uk
Website: www.pen-and-sword.co.uk

Front Cover: Robert Stephenson & Hawthorn 0-6-0ST 7673 shunts Foxfield Colliery yard on 21 July 2012 whilst visiting the Foxfield Steam Railway as 'guest' loco during a weekend Gala event.
Back Cover: Bagnall 0-6-0ST 2572 'Judy' leads Bagnall 0-6-0ST 3058 'Alfred' down Foxfield Bank on 7 April 2013 with a rake of wagons to form a freight service that was part of the Foxfield Steam Railway's event programme during a gala weekend.

Contents

The history of steam locomotives within the United Kingdom is normally described in terms of those locomotives which were built for, and operated on, the main lines that ultimately became nationalised in 1948 as British Railways (BR). Whilst this covers a large part of the UK's railway history, it also overlooks the major role played within many UK companies which also operated railways – with equally dedicated steam locomotives.

This was the heartlands of British Industry where companies used railways as an internal resource in the production of goods, whether by bringing the raw materials to the point of production, shunting materials during the course of production or by moving finished goods to an interchange siding to be transferred to train services operating on the national network.

The main-line companies became sufficiently large that they were able to build their own locomotives specifically designed to work their train services whilst industrial companies were obliged to buy their locomotives from builders who offered a wide range of designs that covered the diverse range of tasks which were to be found within industrial operations.

This market gave rise to a number of companies whose products fuelled the initial impetus of the Industrial Revolution but this began to dissipate during the early part of the 20th century leading to mergers and company name changes. The pressure increased further during that century as petrol engined, then later diesel engined, traction was developed and many locomotive builders found themselves unable to compete and thus went into liquidation.

The mass withdrawal of steam locomotives from BR during the 1960s, as it converted to 'modern' diesel and electric traction, led to a preservation movement that concentrated on saving as many locomotives as possible. The parallel withdrawal of steam locomotives in industrial use, however, due to the closure of companies or their re-organisation leading to increasing use of alternative transport, was recorded by few enthusiasts and the preservation of working examples undertaken by even fewer.

It is to the credit of many heritage lines, unable to afford the rising prices of main-line steam locomotives or the effort required to restore many rescued from scrap lines and scrap yards, that they continued developing their lines by turning to industrial steam locomotives as a first stage in starting up. By the beginning of the 21st century many heritage lines had at least one example in their fleets and some centres were quite happy to operate services at a level where the industrial locomotive(s) were able to operate the timetabled services.

This resulted in a large variety of locomotive types still being operated in the 21st century and keeping alive the name of many companies, many no longer in business, which once formed an important group of engineering skills that supplied steam locomotives to the world.

This album is dedicated to those builders whose products are still in use many years after being built and, whilst not an authoritative collection, seeks to give a sample of the best of UK-built Industrial Steam Locomotives.

Fred Kerr
December 2016

Opposite: Andrew Barclay 0-4-0ST 1147 'John Howe' powers over the Marina Bridge in Preston Marina complex on 18 February 2012 whilst working a Ribble Steam Railway shuttle service.

AB: Andrew Barclay Sons & Company

1147 hauls a Riversway–Strand Rd shuttle alongside the Riverside Walk, adjacent to the River Ribble, on 17 September 2011.

Date Established
1864

Location
Caledonia Works, Kilmarnock

History
The company's owners had been producing locomotives since 1832 but their earlier companies had gone into administration. The 1864 company finally succeeded and produced many steam locomotives, including some to the designs of these earlier companies, as well as designing 'fireless' locomotives and diesel locomotives. In 1972 the company was taken over by the Hunslet Engine Company but subsequent takeovers and amalgamations saw it become part of the USA-owned Wabtec Group of companies in 2015; its main activity thereafter was geared to coaching stock repairs and modifications.

0-4-0ST 1147 'John Howe' was built in 1908 to the order of Howe's Plaster Works located near Cumwhinton in Cumbria but, as at 2015, it is preserved by the Ribble Steam Railway located in the Preston Dock complex.

1147 shunts stock at the shed during an evening photo charter on 5 February 2010.

The Ribble Steam Railway includes a Museum wherein it displays locomotives which are either awaiting restoration or are surplus to requirements but worthy of retaining for display purposes. Included in the collection are a number of Barclay 0-4-0ST locomotives, including:

Right: 1598 'Efficient', delivered to McKechnie Brothers copper smelting works at St Helens in 1918, being displayed on 17 September 2011.

Below Left: 1969 'J.N. Derbyshire', delivered to Carlisle Plaster & Cement Company of Cumwhinton in 1929, being displayed on 23 February 2011.

Below Right: 1865 'Alexander', delivered to Southall Gas Works in 1926, being displayed on 23 February 2011.

Above: 0-6-0T 1245 was supplied to the Carron Iron Company of Falkirk in 1911; as at 2016 it is preserved at the Lakeside & Haverthwaite Railway where it was stabled in Haverthwaite shed on 6 March 2015.

The Ribble Steam Railway has a comprehensive workshops facility where:

Top Right: 0-4-0ST 2261, supplied to the National Coal Board in 1949, is now resident and where it was noted being overhauled in the workshop facility on 23 February 2011.

Bottom Right: Being displayed in the shed yard on 18 February 2012 prior to being repainted.

OPPOSITE PAGE

Top Left: The company was one of the largest builders of fireless locomotives, building 114 examples between 1913–1961, with an example, 0-4-0F 1950 'Heysham No. 2', being displayed in the Ribble Steam Railway's museum on 17 September 2011.

Bottom Left: 0-4-0ST 2134 was supplied to British Gypsum in 1942 and was a display item at the Open Day held by the West Coast Railway Company at its Carnforth site on 26 July 2008.

Right: 0-6-0T 1605 'Ajax' was supplied to the Harlaxton Quarries (by Grantham) in 1918 but as at 2015 is now preserved at the Isle of Wight Steam Railway where it was displayed at its Haven Street base on 8 June 2010.

The company was sub-contracted during World War II to build locomotives to the Hunslet Engine Company Class 50555 0-6-0ST design (see **HE: Hunslet Engine Company**); this design was more commonly referred to as the 'Austerity' Class and class members as 'Austerities'.

Top Left: Working the stock of a Bury–Ramsbottom shuttle service from the station into the siding.

Bottom Left: Crossing Burrs Common whilst working a Bury–Ramsbottom shuttle service.

0-6-0ST 2183 was supplied to the War Department in 1943 as WD71529; it was sold to the Wemyss Private Railway (Fife) in 1964 where it became fleet number 15 and, when the railway closed, 2183 was bought by T Muir of Kirkcaldy for scrap in 1970. It remained in long term storage until bought privately in 2003 to enter preservation and subsequently moving to the Gloucestershire Warwickshire Railway in 2007. A later move was made to the East Lancashire Railway where it was overhauled before being transferred to the Avon Valley Railway in March 2013 where it remains as at 2015. A visit to the ELR on 24 January 2009 saw the locomotive:

Top Right: 0-4-0ST 2315 'Lady Ingrid' was supplied to the South of Scotland Electricity Board's Braehead Power Station in 1951 and was noted under repair at the Tunbridge Wells West workshops of the Spa Valley Railway on 17 June 2011.

Bottom: 0-6-0T 2017 was supplied to the Wemyss Bay Private Railway in 1935 and entered preservation at the Strathspey Railway where, on 18 August 2007, it was noted passing Drumuillie with a Broomhill–Aviemore service.

Ae: Avonside Engine Company

Date Established
1837

Location
Bristol

History
The firm began business as Henry Stothert and Company in 1837 and operated under various names until 1864 when the company took advantage of the Companies Act to become the Avonside Engine Company.

The company entered voluntary liquidation in 1934; the goodwill and designs of the company were bought in 1935 by the Hunslet Engine Company.

0-4-0T 1977 *Cadbury No 1* was supplied to Cadbury's Bournville Works Railway in 1925 from where it entered preservation in February 1963 with the Dowty Railway Preservation Society based at Ashchurch.

Left: 0-4-0T 1977 was a display item at Tyseley Locomotive Works on 24 June 2012 during a site Open Day whilst earlier

Right: it had been stored at the Toddington base of the Gloucestershire Warwickshire Railway on 30 May 2010.

0-4-0ST 1498 'Desmond' was supplied to Orb Steelworks in 1906; it was noted being overhauled in the workshops of the Llangollen Railway on 12 December 2010.

0-6-0ST 1568 'Lucy' was supplied to the Hutchinson Estate and Dock Company in 1909 to work in Widnes Docks. It was withdrawn from service in January 1971 and entered preservation in February 1972 when bought by the Liverpool Locomotive Preservation Group and moved to storage in a dockside engine shed at Seacombe. It subsequently moved to the Steamport Museum at Southport on 1 August 1973 and is now resident at the Ribble Steam Railway where it was noted as a display item in the museum on 17 September 2011.

Bag: W.G. Bagnall & Company

Date Established
1875

Location
Stoke on Trent

History
The firm was founded in 1875 when William G Bagnall took over the firm of Massey & Hill and manufactured agricultural machinery, colliery plant and engineer's requirements. He built his first locomotive in 1876 and in 1887 the company was renamed W.G. Bagnall Ltd. In 1951 the company was sold to become Brush-Bagnall Traction Ltd as an associate company of Brush Electrical Engineering based at Loughborough. The company subsequently changed ownership many times; by 1962 it was owned by Dorman Diesels and when this latter company was taken over by English Electric Company Ltd in 1962, locomotive building ceased completely.

0-6-0ST 2221 'Lewisham' was supplied to the Shropshire Beet Sugar Company site at Alscott (near Wellington) in 1927 and entered preservation at the Foxfield Steam Railway (FSR) in 1970.

Right: 2221 forms a display item in the FSR museum, located at its Caverswall Road base, on 9 August 2014 whilst awaiting overhaul.

Bottom: 2221 stands in the yard at the FSR's Caverswall Road base on 7 April 2013.

0-4-0ST 2572 'Judy' was one of 2 locomotives (0-4-0ST 3058 'Alfred' being the other) supplied in 1937 and 1952 respectively to Par Docks where the restricted height of the site called for a peculiar design. 2572 was withdrawn from service in 1969 and was subject to periods of storage and display before entering preservation with the Cornish Steam Locomotive Preservation Society (CSLPS) in 2004 at the Bodmin & Wenford Railway (BWR). It joined 3058 which had worked until 1977 before entering preservation with the CSLPS at its Bugle site before moving to the BWR in 1987. Both locomotives are now based at the BWR from where they make occasional visits as a pair to other heritage railway sites.

During September 2012 the duo visited the Swanage Railway as the 'guest' locomotives for its Autumn Steam Gala during which, on 9 September.

Right and Bottom: 2572 'Judy' powered a Motola–Norden shuttle service in top 'n mode with 3058 'Alfred' using Class 108 trainset 54504 + 51933.

The rear of the shuttle train was provided by 3058 'Alfred' here seen crossing the road on its approach to Norden on 9 September 2012 with one of the shuttle services formed of Class 108 trainset 51933 + 54504.

The duo later suffered failures on 9 September 2012 and were moved into the siding at Norden to facilitate inspection and repair. The consist in the siding comprised 3058 'Alfred' + 2572 'Judy' + Class 108 trainset 54504 + 51933.

In April 2013 the duo visited the Foxfield Steam Railway as the 'guest' locomotives for the line's Spring Steam Gala; scenes from the event on 7 April 2013 included:

Opposite Top: 2572 'Judy' leading 3058 'Alfred' down Foxfield Bank with a rake of wagons to form a freight service that was part of the event programme.

Opposite Bottom: 3058 'Alfred' leading 2572 'Judy' as they assemble a freight train.

Above: 3058 'Alfred' leading 2572 'Judy' as they ascend Foxfield Bank with a Foxfield Colliery–Dilhorne Park Demonstration Freight train.

The normal arrangement for locomotive workings during Foxfield Steam Railway Gala events is that a locomotive works a Demonstration Freight train from Foxfield Colliery to Dilhorne Park where it then changes places with another locomotive to work the returning Dilhorne Park–Caverswall Road passenger service before reversing the arrangement to return to Foxfield Colliery.

Top: 3058 'Alfred' leads 2572 'Judy' out of Foxfield Colliery with a Demonstration Freight train to Dilhorne Park.

Bottom: 3058 'Alfred' pilots 2572 'Judy' into Caverswall Road with a passenger service from Dilhorne Park.

Opposite Page: Bagnall diesel locomotive 3150 'Wolstanton No. 3' provides rear-end assistance as 3058 'Alfred' leads 2572 'Judy' out of Foxfield Colliery with a Demonstration Freight train to Dilhorne Park.

OPPOSITE PAGE

Left: 2842 climbs out of Foxfield Colliery on 7 April 2013 with a Demonstration Freight train to Dilhorne Park.

Right: 2842 descends Foxfield Bank on its approach to Foxfield Colliery on 18 July 2015 with a Demonstration Freight train from Dilhorne Park.

0-4-0ST 2842 was supplied to the Kent Electric Power Company in 1942 who based it at Littlebrook Power Station in Dartford. It was bought privately for preservation in November 1972 and moved to the Mid-Hants Railway in July 1973; as at 2016 it is based at the Foxfield Steam Railway in Staffordshire.

CURRENT PAGE

Below: 2842 is banked by 0-4-0CT 4101 on 20 July 2013 as it climbs out of Foxfield Colliery with a Demonstration Freight train to Dilhorne Park.

Left: 0-6-0ST 2682 'Princess' was supplied to Preston Corporation in 1942 and fitted with steam heat to heat the banana vans which carried the fruit, imported through the port, throughout the country. It was initially preserved at the Lakeside & Haverthwaite Railway, where it was seen departing from Newby Bridge on 17 April 2006 whilst working a Lakeside–Haverthwaite service, but as at 2016 it is based at the Ribble Steam Railway from where it is hired to heritage lines.

Top Right: 0-6-0ST 2680 was the first of its class and was supplied to Birchenwood Gas and Coke Company in 1942 named 'Birchenwood No 4'. The site closed in May 1973 and 2680 entered preservation with Sir Robert McAlpine at his Market Overton base; following several changes of owners it is now based at the Ribble

Steam Railway where it has adopted the guise of Preston Docks 'Courageous' as seen on 15 February 2014 when it was posed as part of an evening photo charter.

Bottom Right: 0-4-0ST 2842 shunts a freight train at the Foxfield Steam Railway's Caverswall Road on 7 April 2013.

CURRENT PAGE

Below: 0-6-0ST 3059 'Florence No 2' was supplied to the National Coal Board (North Staffs area) in 1954 and, as at 2016, it is preserved at the Foxfield Steam Railway where it was noted on 20 July 2013 climbing out of Foxfield Colliery with a Demonstration Freight train to Dilhorne Park.

Opposite Page: 3059 climbs out of Foxfield Colliery on 7 April 2013 with a Foxfield Colliery–Dilhorne Park Demonstration Freight train.

Left: 3059 curves onto Foxfield Bank as it leaves the colliery yard on 12 October 2013 with a Foxfield Colliery–Dilhorne Park Demonstration Freight train.

Bottom: 3059 banks a Foxfield Colliery–Dilhorne Park Demonstration Freight train out of Foxfield Colliery on 20 July 2013, whilst Dubs 0-4-0CT 4101 awaits its next duty.

Left: 3059 curves onto Foxfield Bank on 21 July 2012 with a Foxfield Colliery–Dilhorne Park Demonstration Freight train.

Top: 3059 banks a Foxfield Colliery–Dilhorne Park Demonstration Freight train out of the colliery on 18 July 2015.

0-6-0ST 2668 'Cranford No 2' was supplied to the Cranford Ironstone Quarry (Northamptonshire) in 1942. As at 2016 it is based at the Rutland Railway Museum but was once resident at the Embsay & Bolton Abbey Railway where:

Top Right: It awaited departure from Embsay on 1 January 2002 with a service to Bolton Abbey.

Bottom Right: It formed a Demonstration Freight train from Bolton Abbey to Embsay on 15 October 2005 during an Autumn Steam Gala.

0-4-0ST 2648 was supplied to the Ministry of Supply in 1940, being the first of 9 locomotives built for use in Royal Ordnance factories; as at 2016 it is based at the Ribble Steam Railway in Preston where, on 12 February 2011:

Bottom Left: It piloted Hunslet Engine Company 0-6-0ST 3155 over the Marina Bridge whilst working a Strand Road–Riversway shuttle service.

Date Established
1865

Location
Gateshead

History
The firm was founded in 1865 when the works of R. Coulthard & Company, which had gone into liquidation, were take over by William Black and Thomas Hawthorn. The firm ceased trading in 1896 after building over 1100 locomotives but the company was bought by Chapman & Furneaux who continued building a further

70 locomotives before ceasing to trade in 1902. The goodwill, drawings, patterns and templates were bought by R&W Hawthorn Leslie and Company Ltd in 1902.

The sole surviving example of a locomotive built by Black Hawthorn is 0-4-0ST 305 which is, as at 2016, currently displayed in the National Rail Museum at York where the following images were taken on:

Left: 06 July 2008.

Below: 12 November 2005.

Bottom Right: 11 May 2007.

Bor: E. Borrows & Sons

Date Established
1865

Location
St Helens

History
The firm was founded in 1865 by Edward Borrows who commenced building 0-4-0 locomotives fitted with a well-tank that were sold mainly to local companies in Lancashire. The locomotive business was taken over in 1910 by H.W. Johnson and Company and a further 3 Borrows-type locomotives were built by the latter company between 1913 and 1921.

There are only 3 surviving examples of the Borrows 0-4-0ST well-tank design, of which 2 are located at the Ribble Steam Railway. Number 53 'Windle' was supplied to Pilkington Brothers in 1909 for use in their glasswork factory sites at St Helens. The company initially donated it to the Middleton Railway Preservation Society but, following a series of transfers, the locomotive moved to the Ribble Steam Railway in December 2010 where, as at 2016, it was being restored in the workshop facility.

Progress on the overhaul is noted at *Left* on 2 April 2011 and *Right* on 18 February 2012.

The 2nd of the 2 locomotives in the care of the Ribble Steam Railway is Number 48 'King' which was supplied to Pilkington Brothers of St Helens . The company initially operated it in their London works before returning it to St Helens, from where it entered preservation with the Industrial Preservation Group in spring 1967.

As at 2016, the locomotive is on display in the Ribble Steam Railway's Museum where it was photographed on:

Top Left: 17 September 2011.

Bottom Left: 23 February 2011.

Bottom Right: 11 January 2004.

BP: Beyer Peacock & Company

Date Established
1864

Location
Gorton, Manchester

History
The firm was founded in 1864 by Charles Beyer and Richard Peacock and initially built locomotives for both railway companies and industrial concerns. It also developed an export trade but gained greatest fame by the creation of the 'Garratt' articulated locomotive design, many of which were exported. Although it adapted to build diesel locomotives during the late 1950s / early 1960s, the change came too late and the company entered voluntary liquidation in 1966.

There are few examples of Beyer Peacock locomotives in preservation but the Foxfield Steam Railway operates 0-4-0ST 1827 which was originally built in 1879 with a crane unit and operated as a works shunter for Beyer Peacock at its Gorton site. The date of conversion to a 'normal' locomotive is unknown but on closure of the company the locomotive entered preservation in 1966 when donated to the fledgling Foxfield Steam Railway.

Bottom Left: 1827 departs from Foxfield Colliery on 18 July 2015 working a Demonstration Freight train to Dilhorne Park, with rear-end support from Dubs 0-4-0CT 4101, during a gala weekend.

Bottom Right: 1827 climbs up to Caverswall Road station on 9 August 2014 with a passenger service from Dilhorne Park; the trainset was the vintage North Staffordshire Railway coaches supported by a brake-van to meet modern train-braking requirements.

Manchester's Museum of Science and Industry (MOSI) held a celebration of Beyer Peacock 'survivors' in August 2009 which not only included 0-4-0ST 1827 but a rare example of a Garratt locomotive built for a British industrial operator. Garratt 0-4-4-0 6841 was supplied to Baddesley Colliery in 1937 to work trains to the interchange sidings at Atherstone, adjacent to the West Coast Main Line, and where it was named 'William Francis' after the son of the mine-owner. When the colliery was closed in 1966, 6841 was stored before entering preservation at the Bressingham Garden Centre (near Diss) in 1968.

Top: 1827 poses in MOSI's yard with 6841 'William Francis' on 13 August 2009 during the Beyer Peacock Commemoration.

Bottom: 6841 'William Francis' is seen posed in MOSI's yard on 13 August 2009 during the commemorative event.

Dubs: Dubs & Company

Date Established
1863

Location
Polmadie, Glasgow

History
The firm was founded in 1863 when Henry Dubs left his position as managing partner with Nielson & Company to form his own business. The company built many locomotives, including the creation of the crane tank design, but in 1903 it amalgamated with the local firms of Neilson Reid and Company and Sharp Stewart and Company to form the North British Locomotive Company [see **NBL = North British Locomotive Company**]. The Dubs site at Polmadie was renamed Queens Park Works and retained its diamond-shaped works plate within the new partnership.

Few examples of the company's products remain in existence but a rare example of a Crane Tank is preserved at the Foxfield Steam Railway in Staffordshire where 0-4-0CT 4101 is located. It was built in 1901 and supplied to the Shelton Iron & Steel Works where it worked until 1968. Initially bought by enthusiasts and moved to the East Somerset Railway at Cranmore for restoration and preservation, it was withdrawn for overhaul in 1986. The work was never completed and the locomotive was offered to Foxfield in order to return it to its spiritual home in Staffordshire. The locomotive is now a popular sight at gala events where its activities include:

Left: setting up a Demonstration Freight train in the colliery yard at Foxfield on 18 July 2015.

Bottom: banking a Foxfield Colliery–Dilhorne Park Demonstration Freight train up Foxfield Bank on 20 July 2013.

4101 normally banks Foxfield Colliery–Dilhorne Park Demonstration Freight trains as shown at *Top Left/Top Right* on 20 July 2013. Its crane-lifting ability is often demonstrated during Gala events, as shown at *Bottom Left* on 21 July 2012 and *Bottom Right* on 18 July 2015.

GR: Grant Ritchie & Company

Date Established
1876

Location
Townsend Works, Kilmarnock

History
The firm was founded in 1876 when Thomas Grant and William Ritchie left Andrew Barclay after a disastrous fire at the latter company's premises and took over the business of Grant Brothers. The new company sold machinery to the mining industry, including locomotives, but little else is known of the company which ceased trading in 1920.

0-4-0ST 272 is one of only 2 surviving locomotives (the other being 0-4-2ST 536 now preserved at the Prestongrange Museum, East Lothian) and was supplied to the Fife Coal Company in 1894 for service at Kinglassie Colliery. Its final location was at Rothes Colliery from where it moved to Thomas Muir's scrapyard at Easterbalbeggie on 25 November 1969. After long-term storage the locomotive moved to Shrewsbury from where it was moved to the Ribble Steam Railway (RSR) on 22 July 2004 for long-term restoration.

The restoration of 272 was finally completed during 2016 and included the manufacture of many missing components. Its first public appearance was during the RSR's Autumn Steam Gala held in September 2016 and on 11 September 2016 272 was the rear locomotive of the 10:15 Riversway–Strand Road Vintage Train shuttle that was worked in top 'n tail mode with Bagnall 2680 0-6-0ST 'Courageous' as the consist left Riversway's platform.

HC: Hudswell Clarke & Company

Date Established
1860

Location
Jack Lane, Hunslet, Leeds

History
The firm was founded in 1860 as Hudswell and Clarke but renamed to Hudswell, Clarke and Rogers in 1870 then to Hudswell, Clarke in 1881. The company remained in business until 1972 when it was taken over by Hunslet Engine Company in an amalgamation that also included Andrew Barclay Sons and Company of Kilmarnock.

The company built many contractors' locomotives that were designed to be used by contractors for large projects which, once completed, saw the locomotives being sold on to be engaged in further large projects. An example of this is 0-4-0ST 402 'Lord Mayor' which was sold to Edward Nutall of Salford in 1893. Its final owner was George Cohen of Stanningley who sold the loco to the Lord Mayor's Trust in 1968 which moved it to the nascent Dinting Heritage Centre. It was subsequently bought by the Vintage Carriage Trust (VCT) in 1990 and moved to the VCT base at Ingrow on the Keighley & Worth Valley Railway.

Top: 402 is a display item at the National Rail Museum's York site on 12 November 2005.

Bottom: 402 stands in Ingrow yard on 19 February 2006 during a gala event on the Keighley & Worth Valley Railway.

0-6-0ST 1700 'Wissington' was supplied to the nascent British Sugar Corporation in 1938 for service at the Wissington site and remained in East Anglia to become the last commercially-owned steam locomotive in the region. It was bought by the Midland & Great Northern Junction Railway Society and moved to Sheringham in 1978. It then had a lengthy period in storage until restoration began in the late 1990s, leading to a return to service in July 2012 on the North Norfolk Railway followed by a move on loan to the Mid-Suffolk Light Railway, which is the locomotive's current home base as at 2016.

0-6-0ST 1700 rarely leaves the Mid-Suffolk line but in July 2015 it was the guest locomotive at the Foxfield Steam Railway's Summer Gala, where the following series of photographs were taken on 18 July.

1700 'Wissington' + Haydock Foundry 0-6-0WT 'Bellerophon' set up a Demonstration Freight train in the Foxfield Colliery sidings.

OPPOSITE PAGE

Left: 1700 'Wissington' climbs out of Foxfield Colliery with a Foxfield Colliery–Dilhorne Park Demonstration Freight train.

Right: 1700 'Wissington' climbs out of Foxfield Colliery with a Foxfield Colliery–Dilhorne Park Demonstration Freight train.

CURRENT PAGE

Above: 1700 'Wissington' pilots Haydock Foundry 0-6-0WT 'Bellerophon' as they leave Foxfield Colliery with a Demonstration Freight service to Dilhorne Park that has Bagnall 0-6-0ST 3059 'Florence No. 2' providing rear end assistance when the consist passes Dubs 0-4-0CT 4101 stabled in the headshunt.

Left: 1700 'Wissington' sets up its Demonstration Freight train in Foxfield Colliery yard.

Bottom Left: 1700 'Wissington' leaves Foxfield Colliery with a Demonstration Freight train to Dilhorne Park.

Bottom Right: 1700 'Wissington' ascends Foxfield Bank with a Foxfield Colliery – Dilhorne Park Demonstration Freight train to Dilhorne Park.

The Manchester Ship Canal (MSC) once operated a major railway network needing 70 locomotives to service the freight traffic and many locomotives were supplied by Hudswell Clarke. A pair of locomotives have entered preservation, including:

Top: 0-6-0T 679 that was supplied to the MSC in 1903 and became fleet number 31 'Hamburg'. It entered preservation at the Keighley & Worth Valley Railway in June 1967 but traffic growth has seen the locomotive transferred to Oxenhope Museum where it is now a static exhibit as exemplified on 16 August 2014.

Bottom: 0-6-0T 1464 was supplied to the MSC in 1921 and became fleet number 70. It entered preservation at the East Lancashire Railway where it gained the name 'Phoenix' in 1981. It has subsequently been sold on and as at 2016 is reported to be awaiting restoration at the Swindon & Cricklade Railway. It has spent some time at the Ribble Steam Railway where, on 2 February 2003, it was a display item in the workshop's yard during a visit by members of the Heritage Railway Association.

0-6-0ST 1450 'Dorothy' was supplied to the Appleby-Frodingham (later British Steel Corporation) steelworks at Scunthorpe in 1922 and entered preservation at the Embsay & Bolton Abbey Railway in the 1970s. It remained in store for a lengthy period until the advent of the 'Thomas the Tank' era when it was decided to replace the saddle tanks with side tanks and produce a Thomas the Tank lookalike locomotive.

Top Left: 1450 lies stored at Bolton Abbey on 4 May 2013 awaiting overhaul.

Bottom Left: 1450 in its 'Thomas the Tank' guise is piloted by Hunslet Engine Company 0-6-0ST 3783 'Darfield No 1' as they depart from Embsay with a Santa Special to Bolton Abbey on 6 December 2008.

Bottom Right: 0-6-0ST 1539 'Derek Crouch' is a contractors' locomotive that was initially supplied to Robert McAlpine & Son in 1924 for work in Watford; it was subsequently sold to various contractors until ending up with Derek Crouch, who named the locomotive, in the 1960s for work at the Widderington Colliery in Northumberland. In 1972 it was given on permanent loan to the Nene Valley Valley where it was noted at Wansford on 23 February 2015.

0-6-0ST 1782 is a Class 50555 'Austerity' locomotive designed by the Hunslet Engine Company and built by Hudswell Clarke on that company's behalf in 1945. It was supplied to the War Department as WD71505, then moved to the Longmoor Military Railway (LMR) where it was allocated fleet number LMR118 and given the name 'Brussels'.

The LMR closed in 1970 and when a proposed preservation scheme for the railway and its rolling stock collapsed, 1782 was offered to the Keighley & Worth Valley Railway (KWVR) in 1971. Tests during 1972 suggested a conversion to oil firing and the locomotive provided sterling service until traffic demands resulted in the KWVR operating with larger and more powerful locomotives.

1782 was subsequently placed into store and was an early exhibit in the Oxenholme Museum where it now has a permanent role as there seems little possibility that the locomotive will be steamed in the future.

Top: 1782 on display on 13 June 2010.

Bottom: 1782 on display on 11 October 2013.

0-6-0T 1704 'Nunlow' was supplied to G.T Earle Cement Company in 1938 for duties at its Hope site in the Hope Valley. The company subsequently became part of the Associated Portland Cement Manufacturing Company where 1704 operated until being placed in store during 1964. It entered preservation with the Bahamas Locomotive Society (BLS) in 1969 and moved to the society's base at the Dinting Railway Centre. When the centre closed, 1704 was transferred with the BLS stock to Ingrow on the Keighley & Worth Valley Railway (KWVR) where it is now based.

Scenes of 1704 on KWVR operations include:

OPPOSITE PAGE

Departing from Keighley on 12 February 2010 with a service to Oxenhope.

CURRENT PAGE

Top Right: standing in Haworth Loop on 12 October 2014 awaiting a pilot locomotive whilst working a Keighley–Oxenhope service.

Bottom Right: stabling in Haworth shed on 10 February 2012 awaiting its next duty.

Bottom Left: awaiting departure from Keighley on 26 June 2009 with a shuttle service to Damems.

HE: Hunslet Engine Company

Date Established
1864

Location
Hunslet, Leeds

History
The firm was founded in 1864 by John Towlerton Leather, a contractor who thought there was sufficient trade available despite the presence of 3 other locomotive builders (Hudswell Clarke, Kitson and Manning Wardle) in the vicinity of the new company. Despite the 'competition' there was much co-operation between the 4 companies and the venture proved successful including taking over the goodwill and designs of many small manufacturers during the 20th century as trade declined. This included such luminaries as Andrew Barclay Sons & Company; Avonside Engine Company; North British Locomotive Company; Greenwood & Batley; Hudswell Clarke and Company; John Fowler and Company; Kerr Stuart and Company.

In 2004 the company became part of the LH Group which, itself, was bought by the (USA-based) Wabtec Group and the Hunslet name disappeared from commercial operations although as at 2016 its activities continue at Doncaster, Kilmarnock and Loughborough.

1: Austerity Locomotives
The company became most famous during the 1940s when it produced a design for the War Department that subsequently became known as the 'Austerity' class which, after the war had ended, became a popular locomotive for the major industrial operators such as coal mines and power generating stations.

The origins of the design lay in the 8 Class 50550 0-6-0ST locomotives (HE2411-18) ordered by Stewarts & Lloyds for a proposed new ironstone quarry at Islip in Northamptonshire, after which Hunslet suggested that the Ministry of Supply buy an improved 50550 design for use by the War Department, rather than requisition the LMS 'Jinty' 3F 0-6-0 locomotives then being considered.

The Ministry of Supply agreed and the resulting Class 50555 0-6-0ST design was ordered from 1943 with Hunslet sub-contracting construction to Andrew Barclay & Sons (15); W.G. Bagnall (52); Hudswell Clarke and Company (50); Robert Stephenson & Hawthorns (90) and Vulcan Foundry (50) leading to 377 examples being supplied upto 1947. Further orders were placed in the post-war era by the National Coal Board (77); the Army (14) and steel companies (17) resulting in a total of 485 locomotives being built when production ceased in 1964.

Bagnall 0-4-0ST 2668 'Cranford No 2' awaits the arrival of 'Austerity' 0-6-0ST 3788 'Monkton No 1' with a Demonstration Freight train at Bolton Abbey during an Embsay & Bolton Abbey Railway gala event on 15 October 2005.

Top: The 'Austerity' design emanated from the 8 locomotives (0-6-0STs 2411 – 2418) supplied to Stewarts and Lloyds but re-allocated when the proposed development was aborted. 2414 was transferred to the Ministry of Supply who renumbered it as WD66 and moved it to Long Marston. It was replaced by an 'Austerity' locomotive and moved to store at the Longmoor Military Railway prior to being sold to the Port of London Authority where it worked until 1960. It was sold to the National Coal Board who transferred it to Ackton Hall Colliery at Featherstone where it gained fleet number S112. S112 was stored in the open from Summer 1972 until purchased in 1976 and transferred to the Embsay & Bolton Abbey Railway where, on 4 May 2013, it was stored at Bolton Abbey awaiting restoration.

0-6-0ST 3155 was supplied to the Ministry of Supply as 75105 in 1944 and served in France. After the war it was one of 30 sold to the Dutch Railways, becoming Fleet Number 8815, and served in the coal industry in the late 1970s. Initially repatriated to Steamport Southport Museum it subsequently moved to the Ribble Steam Railway on 16 April 1999 where it was restored to service in time for the 2008 Santa Season.

Bottom Left: 3155 is stabled in the workshops on 18 May 2008 awaiting the final stages of its restoration.

Bottom Right: 3155 crosses onto the Marina Bridge on 23 February 2011 whilst working a Riversway–Strand Rd shuttle service.

3155 'Walkden' curves onto the Riverside straight on 19 February 2012 with a Riversway–Strand Rd shuttle service.

Above: 3155 awaits its next duty on Riverside shed on 2 April 2011.

Right: 3155 'Walkden' drifts off the Marina Bridge on 17 September 2011 with a Riversway–Strand Rd shuttle service as Pecket 0-4-0ST 1749 'Fulstow' provides rear end assistance.

0-6-0ST 3794 was supplied to the Ministry of Supply in 1953 as WD194; it was immediately placed in store as part of a War Reserve at the Longmoor Army Stores Depot but left for Bicester when the Longmoor site closed in 1955. It began work in 1958 but after 10 years was withdrawn for overhaul then immediately placed into store. Within a matter of months it was moved to Shoeburyness where it remained until entering preservation in July 1973 when bought by the Lakeside Railway Society for use on the Lakeside & Haverthwaite Railway. It arrived at Haverthwaite in September 1973 and after undergoing overhaul entered traffic in 1974. 3794 remained active there until 2010 when it moved to the Ribble Steam Railway where it began an overhaul in 2011 that was completed in 2015.

3155 pilots 0-6-0ST 3794 'Cumbria' across the Marina Bridge on 7 February 2010 with a Riversway–Strand Road shuttle assisted in the rear by 56xx Class 0-6-2T 5643.

3158 was supplied to the Ministry of Supply in 1944 as WD75109 and was one of 75 locomotives subsequently sold to the London & North Eastern Railway in 1946 where it was numbered 68009. It remained in BR service until withdrawal in August 1962 and subsequent cutting up at Darlington North Road.

The 68009 identity has now been assumed by 0-6-0ST 3825 (*), supplied to the National Coal Board in 1955 for operation in the Kent area and which entered preservation at the Great Central Railway in November 1981. The locomotive has since operated on numerous lines, the latest being the Stainmore Railway where it was withdrawn from service in 2007 and as at 2015 awaits overhaul.

* When 3825 was being overhauled on the Great Central Railway, the identity '68009' was discovered on the boiler and firebox hence the change of identity at some point during its preservation life.

0-6-0ST 3825 (aka 3158) enters Barrow Hill Display yard on 21 October 2006, bearing its British Railways Class J94 number 68009 as it works the depot shuttle service in top 'n tail mode with Jubilee Class 4-6-0 5690 'Leander'.

0-6-0ST 3163 was supplied to the Ministry of Supply in 1944 as WD75113 then WD 132 in the post-war renumbering. In 1963 Hunslet rebuilt the locomotive with equipment designed by L.D. Porta and allocated a new works number 3885 to the rebuild. It was released to traffic in 1965 and initially hired to Coventry Homefire Plant before returning to store at Hunslet's works. It was sold to the National Coal Board in 1970 for use at its Gresford Colliery and subsequent transfer to Bold Colliery when Gresford closed.

It entered preservation in the 1970s, firstly at Chatterley Whitfield Mining Museum (including a loan to the Swanage Railway) then the South Devon Railway from where it was sold to the Flour Mill in 2009.

Whilst at the Flour Mill 3885 was restored to its original condition as 3163 and livery as WD132 before moving to the East Lancashire Railway where, as at 2016, it currently resides.

A visit to Ramsbottom on 19 May 2012 found the locomotive:

CURRENT PAGE

Top: Arriving with a Heywood–Rawtenstall service.

Bottom: Departing with a Heywood–Rawtenstall service.

OPPOSITE PAGE

3163, in its guise as WD132 'Snapper', pilots 15xx Class 0-6-0PT 1501 into Irwell Vale on 19 October 2013 whilst hauling a Heywood – Rawtenstall service on the East Lancashire Railway.

0-6-0ST 3168 was supplied to the Ministry of Supply as WD75118 in 1944 and became WD134 in the post-war renumbering. It was sold to the National Coal Board for service at Wheldale Colliery from where it entered preservation at the Embsay & Bolton Abbey Railway in the early 1980s. When its boiler certificate ran out in the mid 1990s it was placed into store awaiting overhaul which, as at 2016, has yet to start.

3168 has been stored at Bolton Abbey where it was noted awaiting overhaul on: –

Top: 29 October 2006 in the bay platform as a display item.

Bottom: 4 May 2013 in the storage siding.

0-6-0ST 3694 'Whiston' was supplied to the National Coal Board in 1950 for service at Haydock Colliery and it moved to Bold Colliery in 1961. It was stored there in 1981 after suffering boiler problems and entered preservation at the Foxfield Steam Railway (FSR) where it arrived on 26 March 1983 and is now part of the FSR's fleet.

OPPOSITE PAGE

3694 'Whiston' stands in the FSR shed yard at Caverswall Road on 7 April 2013.

3694 'Whiston' was in action on 12 October 2013 when it worked Demonstration Freight trains out of Foxfield Colliery during a late Autumn Gala; scenes from the day included 3694:

Top: Storming out of Foxfield Yard with a Foxfield Colliery–Dilhorne Park working.

Bottom: Banking a Foxfield Colliery–Dilhorne Park service out of the colliery yard.

OPPOSITE PAGE

Attacking Foxfield Bank with a Foxfield Colliery–Dilhorne Park service.

0-6-0ST 3781 was supplied to the National Coal Board in 1952 for duty at Maesteg Colliery before entering preservation at the Kent & East Sussex Railway in early 1977. It was sold on to the Mid-Hants Railway (MHR) where, in 1994, the 0-6-0ST was converted to an 0-6-0T to become one of the licensed 'Thomas the Tank' locomotives. Although based at Ropley, the locomotive can be found at other heritage lines where it operates as part of a 'Thomas the Tank' event.

Top: **3781 bears the guise of 'Thomas the Tank' whilst stabled on the MHR's Ropley shed on 10 June 2010.**

0-6-0ST 3777 was supplied to the National Coal Board in 1952 for duty in the Stoke area from where it entered preservation at the Churnet Valley Railway in February 1977. The railway proposed overhauling it then giving it a red livery and the name 'Josiah Wedgewood' – a name it lost when later re-liveried as BR Class J94 68030. As at 2016 3777 is based at the Churnet Valley Railway where it awaits overhaul.

Right: **3777 poses in Barrow Hill yard as BR Class J94 68030 on 12 April 2014 during a gala event.**

0-6-0ST 3788 'Monckton No. 1' was supplied to the National Coal Board in 1953 for service at Monckton Colliery. When the colliery closed in 1967 the locomotive was transferred to North Gawber Colliery from where it entered preservation at the Embsay & Bolton Abbey Railway in 1980.

A pair of photographs from the same source image sees 3788 'Monckton No 1' leaving Bolton Abbey on 6 December 2008 with a Santa Service for Embsay.

Left: 3788 'Monckton No. 1' stands at Bolton Abbey on 1 January 2009 awaiting departure for Embsay.

Bottom: 3788 'Monckton No. 1' climbs up Hambleton Bank on 1 January 2009 whilst working a Bolton Abbey –Embsay service.

OPPOSITE PAGE

3788 'Monckton No. 1' storms out of Bolton Abbey on 21 September 2008 with a Demonstration Freight train to Embsay during a gala event.

0-6-0ST 3791 was supplied to the Ministry of Supply in 1953 as WD191 and entered preservation at the Kent & East Sussex Railway (KESR) in February 1972. It subsequently gained fleet number 23 and named 'Holman F. Stephens' in honour of Colonel Stephens, the builder of the original line prior to it becoming part of British Railways in 1948.

Left: 3791, in the guise of KESR 23 'Holman F. Stephens', enters Rolvenden on 15 June 2011 with a Bodiam – Tenterden Town service.

Bottom: 0-6-0ST 3790 was supplied to the Ministry of Supply in 1953 as WD190 and entered preservation at the Colne Valley Railway (CVR) in 1973, where it was noted standing in the CVR's station at Castle Hedingham on 18 August 2004 awaiting departure with the shuttle service around the station yard.

0-6-0ST 3792 was supplied to the Ministry of Supply in 1953 as WD192 to operate on the Longmoor Military Railway. It was stored at Long Marston from 1961 where it received the number WD92 and name 'Waggoner' before being moved to the National Army Museum at Beverley. It moved from there on loan to the Isle of Wight Steam Railway in 2005 but full ownership was transferred to the line in May 2008.

OPPOSITE PAGE

3792 'Waggoner' arrives at Haven St on the Isle of Wight Steam Railway on 8 June 2010 with a Smallbrook – Wootton service.

0-6-0ST 3794 was supplied to the Ministry of Supply in 1953 as WD194 and entered preservation with the Furness Trust based at Haverthwaite on the Lakeside & Haverthwaite Railway in 1974. During its time at Haverthwaite the locomotive was named 'Cumbria' and repainted into Furness Railway red livery in 1994 to commemorate the 150th Anniversary of the Furness Railway. The trust moved to the Ribble Steam Railway in 2009 where 3794 received an overhaul; as at 2016 it is hired out to heritage lines throughout the UK with the Ribble Steam Railway now its home location.

Left: 3794 'Cumbria' enters Haverthwaite on 22 August with a Lakeside–Haverthwaite service.

Bottom: 3794 'Cumbria' prepares for duty at Haverthwaite on 5 November 2005.

OPPOSITE PAGE

3794 'Cumbria' runs onto the Ribble Steam Railway shed during an evening photo charter on 5 February 2010.

OPPOSITE PAGE

3794 'Cumbria' + Hawthorn Leslie 0-6-0ST 3931 form the rear of a Ribble Steam Railway shuttle service from Strand Rd – Riversway on 16 May 2015 as the consist crosses the Marina Bridge behind English Electric 0-6-0DE EE 2160 [ex Dutch Railways NS663].

0-6-0ST 3810 was supplied to the National Coal Board in 1954 for service in Welsh Collieries and entered preservation at the Avon Valley Railway from Hafodyrynys Colliery in 1973. It moved to the South Devon Railway in 1978 where, as at 2016, it is still based.

Right: 3810 'Glendower' lies stabled in the Buckfastleigh yard of the South Devon Railway on 22 June 2012.

0-6-0ST 3798 was supplied to the Ministry of Supply in 1953 as WD198 and served at many sites before arriving at Long Marston where it was named 'Royal Engineer' during the 1970s. It entered preservation in 1991 when loaned to the Isle of Wight Steam Railway pending the creation of a Royal Corps of Transport museum at Chatham Dockyard but, when this plan fell through, the loan was converted to a permanent move.

Bottom: 3798 retains its identity as WD198 'Royal Engineer' whilst stabled in the Haven St shed of the Isle of Wight Steam Railway on 12 March 2011.

0-6-0ST 3839 was supplied to the National Coal Board in 1956 for service at Cannock Wood Colliery from where it was withdrawn in the early 1970s to provide a source of spares. It entered preservation in 1973 when bought by an enthusiast who moved it to the Foxfield Steam Railway where, as at 2016, it is still based.

OPPOSITE PAGE

Left: 3839 'Wimblebury' climbs out of Foxfield Colliery on 20 July 2013 with a Demonstration Freight train to Dilhorne Park during a gala event.

Right: 3839 'Wimblebury' climbs out of Foxfield Colliery on 12 October 2013 with a Demonstration Freight train to Dilhorne Park during a gala event.

CURRENT PAGE

Top: 3839 'Wimblebury' climbs out of Foxfield Colliery on 20 July 2013 with a Demonstration Freight train to Dilhorne Park during a gala event.

Bottom: 3839 'Wimblebury' banks a Foxfield Colliery–Dilhorne Park Demonstration Freight train out of Foxfield Colliery on 12 October 2013 during a gala event.

Top Left: 0-6-0ST 3850 'Juno' was supplied to Stewarts & Lloyds Minerals in 1962 to work in its ironstone quarries in the Grantham area; when they closed in 1968 the locomotive was stored. It entered preservation in 1969 with the Ivatt Steam Trust who moved it to Quainton Road then it was transferred to the Isle of Wight Railway in 2009 as part of a deal involving the group's pair of Ivatt Class 2 2-6-2Ts (41298 / 41313). It was subsequently loaned to the NRM's Shildon site as a display item where it was noted on 13 September 2011.

0-6-0ST 3844 is thought to be an alias for 3846 which was supplied to the National Coal Board in 1956 for service in the West Wales area. It was withdrawn from Graig Merthyr Colliery at Pontardulais in the mid 1970s and entered preservation at the Cefn Coed Steam Centre. It subsequently moved to the Appleby-Frodingham site of the Appleby-Frodingham Railway Preservation Society where the owner painted it into the red livery of the United Steel Company and applied the (false) workplates originally applied to 3844. The locomotive was subsequently loaned to the Nene Valley Railway for an indefinite period, where it remains as at 2016.

Bottom Left: 3844 stands in the Nene Valley Railway's Wansford shed yard on 23 February 2015.

Bottom Right: 3844 stands in the Nene Valley Railway's Wansford shed yard on 1 November 2013.

2: Industrial Locomotives

Although the Hunslet Engine Company became most famous during the 1940s when it produced a design for the War Department that subsequently became known as the 'Austerity' class, it had already established a reputation for quality with its range of industrial locomotives which were similar in appearance to the products of the neighbouring firms of Hudswell Clarke, Kitson and Manning Wardle. Most of these locomotives were 0-6-0 tank designs, both saddle and side tank variants, and examples of these are shown in this section.

A pair of Hunslets at the Embsay & Bolton Abbey Railway's Embsay station on 6 December 2008 sees (from left to right) 0-6-0ST 3788 'Monckton No 1' standing at the platform whilst 0-6-0ST 3783 'Darfield No 1' pilots Hudswell Clarke 0-6-0T 1450 (in the guise of Thomas the Tank') as they await departure with a Santa Special to Bolton Abbey.

0-6-0ST 1873 was supplied to the steel firm of Guest Keen and Nettlefold in August 1938 and delivered to its East Moors site in Cardiff. When withdrawn in 1965 it was presented to Cardiff and displayed in Splott Park near to the steelworks. In 1979 it was offered for sale and the purchaser moved it to the Dean Forest Railway in February 1980 and began its restoration. When the owner subsequently moved to Llangollen the restoration was also transferred to Llangollen in 1998 thus allowing the owner to complete the work in December 2003. When Fowler 'Jinty' 3F 0-6-0 47298, in the guise of 'Thomas the Tank', failed at the Llangollen Railway, 1873 was converted to take over the role.

OPPOSITE PAGE

Left: 1873 'Jessie' in original guise awaits overhaul in Llangollen shed on 12 December 2010.

Top Right: 1873 in its guise as 0-6-0T 'Thomas the Tank' runs through Llangollen station on 7 August 2007 with a station shuttle service.

Bottom Right: 1873 'Jessie' in its guise as 0-6-0T 'Thomas the Tank' enters Carrog on 1 March 2015 with a Llangollen–Corwen East service on the day of the official opening of the extension between Carrog and Corwen.

CURRENT PAGE

Right: 1873 'Jessie' acts as Llangollen shed pilot on 10 March 2007.

0-6-0T 686 was supplied to the Manchester Ship Canal in December 1898 as 14 'St Johns' where it worked until 1963. It was then sold to Levenstein for use at its Blakely dyestuffs site in Manchester and where it received the red company livery then named to commemorate the company chairman's wife. When the traffic was transferred to road in 1968 the locomotive was bought by the Warwickshire Industrial Railway Preservation Group and moved to the Severn Valley Railway (SVR) where it was subsequently modified to appear as 'Thomas the Tank'; as at 2016 it has been restored to its Blakely condition for display in the Engine House.

Bottom: 686 'The Lady Armaghdale' is displayed in the SVR's Engine House Museum at Highley on 10 March 2013 whilst awaiting overhaul at Bridgnorth.

Right: 0-6-0ST 1953 'Jacks Green' was supplied to Naylor Benson & Company in September 1939 to work in its Nassington Ironstone Quarry and was one of the last 2 operating steam locomotives in East Anglia when the quarry closed in 1970. 1953 entered preservation with the Peterborough Railway Society (PRS), then based at the local sugar beet factory. When the PRS later devolved into the Nene Valley Railway, 1953 was part of the subsequent move to Wansford. As at 2016, 1953 sees little use and is now a display item at Wansford as photographed on 23 February 2015 when posed on the turntable.

Left: 0-6-0ST 1954 'Kinsley' was supplied to South Kirkby Featherstone and Hemsworth Collieries in December 1939 and was withdrawn from service at South Kirby colliery in 1974 when merry-go-round working of coal trains began. It then entered preservation at the Southport Steamport Museum and was moved to the Preston site of the Ribble Steam Railway (RSR) on 1 April 1999. The locomotive was noted in the RSR workshops on 17 September 2011 whilst undergoing overhaul.

Right: 0-6-0ST 1982 'Ring Haw' was sold to Naylor Benson & Company to work in its Nassington Ironstone Quarry and was one of the last 2 operating steam locomotives in East Anglia when the quarry closed in 1970. 1982 entered preservation at the North Norfolk Railway shortly after but as at 2016 it is on loan to the Nene Valley Railway where it was photographed on 23 February 2015 stabled in Wansford shed yard.

0-6-0ST 2705 'Beatrice' was supplied to Ackton Hall Colliery in August 1945 and remained there until the colliery closed in 1985. 2705 entered preservation shortly after at the Embsay & Bolton Abbey Railway where it is still based as at 2015.

Right: **2705 'Beatrice' awaits departure from Embsay on 31 August 2013 with an Embsay–Bolton Abbey service.**

0-6-0ST 2409 'King George' was supplied to the Linby Colliery Company in May 1942, ending service with the National Coal Board at Gedling Colliery in the 1960s. It was sold to contractors but ended in the scrapyard of Jeremy Walker at Witney, Oxon from where it was rescued and entered preservation in June 1981 at the Gloucestershire Warwickshire Railway. 2409 moved to the Didcot Railway Centre in December 2011 and where, in 2016, it is stored awaiting an overhaul.

Bottom: **2409 'King George' sits in Toddington yard of the Gloucestershire Warwickshire Railway on 11 April 2004.**

2705 'Beatrice' storms out of Bolton Abbey on 6 October 2013 with a service to Embsay.

0-6-0ST 3783 'Darfield No. 1' was supplied to the National Coal Board for service at Darfield colliery in September 1953 from where it entered preservation in 1974 with a private buyer then moved to the Embsay & Bolton Abbey Railway. It subsequently moved to Llangollen from where it is hired to other lines, including the Embsay & Bolton Abbey Railway on occasions. Such an occasion occurred on 21 September 2008 when 3783 was noted working a train of vintage vehicles on a Bolton Abbey–Embsay service.

Top Left: 3783 'Darfield No 1' lies stored in Llangollen shed yard on 26 March 2011.
Top Right: 3783 'Darfield No 1' lies stabled in Llangollen yard on 31 May 2008.
Bottom Left: 3783 'Darfield No 1' undergoes disposal at Embsay on 21 September 2008 at the end of its day's duty.
Bottom Right: 3783 'Darfield No 1' awaits departure from Embsay on 1 January 2010 with a service to Bolton Abbey.

HF: Haydock Foundry

Date Established
1868

Location
Haydock

History
The foundry was part of a larger colliery complex at Haydock for which it built machinery including 6 locomotives between 1868–1887. 'Bellerophon' was built in 1874 as Works Number F and survived into the ownership of the National Coal Board. It was withdrawn for scrapping in 1964 but was rescued and entered preservation with the Keighley & Worth Valley Railway. In 1981 the locomotive was bought by the Vintage Carriages Trust and restored to working order; it is a popular locomotive and visits many heritage lines as 'guest' locomotive especially for gala events. As at 2016 'Bellerophon' is on long-term loan to the Foxfield Steam Railway where it is operated as part of that line's North Staffordshire Railway Vintage Train.

Bottom: During a visit to the Keighley & Worth Valley in October 2010, 'Bellerophon' was used on the Lancashire & Yorkshire Railway Vintage Train, here seen departing from Keighley on 9 October with a service to Ingrow.

Scenes of 'Bellerophon' at work on the Foxfield Steam Railway during gala events as it:

OPPOSITE PAGE

Storms out of Foxfield Colliery on 21 July 2012 with a Demonstration Freight train for Dilhorne Park.

CURRENT PAGE

Top: stands at Dilhorne Park with the North Staffordshire Railway Vintage Train on 9 August 2014 awaiting departure to Caverswall Road.

Bottom: attacks Foxfield Bank on 18 July 2015 with a Foxfield Colliery–Dilhorne Park Demonstration Freight train.

NOTE: Dilhorne Park station carries the name 'Hanbury Halt' as used in episodes of the BBC1 TV series 'Cranford' when the railway provided locations for the railway scenes in the programme.

In June 2015 the North Staffordshire Railway Vintage Train made a brief visit to the neighbouring Churnet Valley Railway during which an evening photo charter was arranged. Scenes from that brief visit included 'Bellerophon':

OPPOSITE PAGE

Approaching Consall on 26 June 2015 with a Leek Brook–Froghall service.

CURRENT PAGE

Top: Entering Froghall station during the evening photo charter on 26 June 2015.

Bottom: Posing in Cheddleton station during the photo charter on 26 June 2015.

'Bellerophon' departs from Cheddleton on 27 June 2015 with the first Vintage Train service of the day to Froghall.

HL: R & W Hawthorn, Leslie & Company

Date Established
1886

Location
St Peter's Works, Newcastle

History

The company was formed in 1886 by the merger of shipbuilder A Leslie and Company of Hebburn (established in Aberdeen in 1850; established in Hebburn in 1854) with the locomotive works of R&W Hawthorn of Newcastle (established in 1817 as Robert Hawthorn but renamed to R&W Hawthorn in 1820).

The company divested itself of its locomotives interests in 1937 to Robert Stephenson and Company which subsequently renamed itself Robert Stephenson & Hawthorn Ltd [see **RSH = Robert Stephenson & Hawthorn Ltd**]

Bottom: 0-4-0ST 3715 was supplied to the Associated Portland Cement Company site at Swanscombe in 1928 where it worked until replaced by diesel locomotives in 1969. It was then bought by the Gravesend Railway Enthusiast's Society and moved to the Ashford Steam Centre in October 1972. The site was closed in May 1976 and 3715 was moved to the Colne Valley Railway where it was seen as a display item during a visit to Castle Hedingham on 18 August 2004.

Top Right: 0-4-0ST 2491 was supplied to Websters Brick & Lime Works for service at its Coventry site where it was named 'Rosabel'. In 1926 – as part of an exchange deal – 2491 was sold to British Celanese at Spondon where it was renamed 'Henry' but subsequently moved to the Foleshill factory in Coventry where it was retained as a static exhibit once withdrawn from service. In 1983 restoration began that expanded into restoration to full working order after which it was moved to Tyseley Locomotive Works in 1986. 2491 is now in need of further overhaul and, as at 2016, is a display item in Barrow Hill Roundhouse where it was noted on 29 September 2013.

Bottom Right: 0-4-0ST 3135 'Invincible' was supplied to Woolwich Arsenal in 1915 and worked until placed into store in 1955; it was subsequently overhauled and sent to RAE Farnborough in 1959 where it worked until the system's closure in 1968. It was purchased privately by Tom Jeffris who loaned it to the Isle of Wight Steam Railway (IoWSR) in 1971; on his death in 1979 ownership was passed to the IoWSR where it was noted as a static exhibit on the Haven St forecourt on 8 June 2010.

Bottom Left: 0-6-0ST 3931 was supplied to Stewarts & Lloyds in 1938 to work at the new Corby Steelworks and survived until replaced by diesel traction in June 1973. It entered preservation at the Shackerstone Railway in October 1973 but moved to the Swanage Railway in December 1982 where it gained the name 'Linda'. Subsequent moves to the Gwili Railway and the Ribble Steam Railway saw 3931 return to service in May 2015; here it is crossing the Marina Bridge on 16 May 2015 working in tandem with Hunslet Engineering 0-6-0ST 3794 'Cumbria' on a Strand Road – Riversway shuttle service.

K: Kitson & Company

Date Established
1835

Location
Airedale Works, Hunslet, Leeds

History
The company was started in 1835 as James Kitson but underwent various name changes (Todd, Kitson & Laird; Kitson & Laird; Kitson, Thompson & Hewitson; Kitson & Hewitson) before becoming Kitson and Company in 1863. The company lost custom in the 1920s and called in the receivers in 1934; despite restructuring in 1937 locomotive construction ceased in 1938 whilst the patterns, drawings and goodwill were acquired by Robert Stephenson & Hawthorn although locomotive components were supplied until 1945.

Bottom: 0-6-2T 4263 was the first 0-6-2T design produced by the company and supplied to Lambton Colliery in 1904. It remained there throughout years of merger until the closure of the colliery system in 1969 then entered preservation at the North Yorkshire Moors Railway where it is still based. 4263 is seen passing Esk Cottages on 27 September 2014 as it begins the ascent of Goathland Bank with a Demonstration Freight train from Grosmont to Goathland during the Autumn Steam Gala.

Departing from Consall with a Froghall–
Cheddleton service.

Although 4263 is normally based on the North Yorkshire Moors Railway (NYMR), an appeal by the Churnet Valley Railway in August 2013 for a locomotive loan to overcome a temporary shortage of motive power saw 4263 moving south for a short period. A visit to Consall on 17 August 2013 noted 4263:

Top: approaching Consall with a Froghall – Cheddleton service.

Bottom: Back on home territory 4263 shunts a Demonstration Freight train at Goathland on 27 September 2014 during the NYMR's Autumn Steam Gala.

0-6-0ST 5459 was built to an earlier Manning Wardle design (Kitson having taken over the goodwill of Manning Wardle in 1927 when the latter company became bankrupt) and supplied to the Austin Motor Company to work at the Longbridge site in Birmingham. When withdrawn from service, 5459 was bought in November 1973 by the Burtonwood Brewery on behalf of the Flint & Deeside Railway Society then stored behind the Nant Hotel in Prestatyn until the Society moved to Llangollen in 1975. In recognition of the support from the brewery 5459 initially carried the name 'Burtonwood Brewer'.

5459 has remained at Llangollen from the earliest days of the Llangollen Railway and recent visits have seen the locomotive:

Top: Under repair on 31 May 2008.

Bottom: Under overhaul on 12 December 2010.

KS: Kerr Stuart and Company

Date Established
1881

Location
California Works, Stoke on Trent

History
The company was founded in Glasgow in 1881 as James Kerr & Company to supply railway plant but orders for new locomotives were sub-contracted to Hartley, Arnoux and Fanning of Stoke on Trent; John Fowler of Leeds and Falcon / Brush of Loughborough.

In 1893 James Kerr took over Hartley, Arnoux and Fanning and renamed the company Kerr Stuart and Company and specialised in building small industrial locomotives until 1930 when deteriorating trade conditions saw the company close and the locomotive designs, patterns and goodwill sold to the Hunslet Engine Company.

Top Right: 0-4-0WT 3063 was built in 1918 to an older Borrows locomotive design which dates back to the 1860s. It was supplied to the Admiralty for service at Chepstow but the end of WWI rendered it surplus and it was sold to Fairfield-Mabeys for service at Chepstow. 3063 was placed in store during the 1960s and remained there until bought by Bill Parker and his brother in 1980. Now nicknamed 'Willy', 3063 was restored to working order and is based at Bill Parker's Flour Mill workshops where it is available for hire as on 20 July 2013 when it was setting up a Demonstration Freight train at Foxfield colliery whilst appearing at a Foxfield Steam Railway Summer Gala as the 'guest locomotive'.

Bottom Right: 0-4-0ST 4388 was supplied in 1926 to the British Gas Light Company at Etruria until replaced by diesel locomotives in 1949 and being sold to Brookfield Foundry & Engineering based in the old Kerr Stuart works. The works ceased rail traffic in 1962 and 4388 was stored on site until 1982 when the company went into liquidation. At the subsequent asset sale 4388 was bought privately and moved to the Foxfield Steam Railway (FSR) where it is still located. On a visit to the FSR on 20 July 2013, 4388 was noted stored awaiting overhaul.

MW: Manning Wardle & Company

Date Established
1858

Location
Boyne Engine Works, Leeds

History
The firm was created from the remnants of E.B. Wilson and Company whose affairs had been looked after by Alexander Campbell on the death of E.B. Wilson in 1856. When the works closed down, Alexander Campbell received finance in 1858 from a local vicar named Wardle to establish a new company; further finance was needed and this was provided by John Manning and the new company took the name 'Manning Wardle'. The company bought the drawings and patterns of E.B. Wilson and the first locomotives were based on these.

Manning Wardle was based in Jacks Lane where, subsequently, the firms of Hudswell, Clarke & Company and Hunslet Engine Company established their business thus leading Manning Wardle to build locomotives for contractors and industrial use. The company failed to adapt sufficiently to the post-WWI conditions and ceased trading in 1927 with its assets being acquired by Kitson who produced further Manning Wardle-designed locomotives until the latter's demise in 1938; the patterns passed to Robert Stephenson & Hawthorn [see **RSH = Robert Stephenson & Hawthorn**] who produced a further 5 locomotives to the early Manning Wardle designs.

0-6-0ST 1210 was supplied in 1891 to Logan & Hemingway, a firm of contractors building the Manchester, Sheffield & Lincolnshire Railway (later the Great Central Railway), and continued at work with that company until its liquidation in 1935 when 1210 was sold to the Cranford Ironstone Company where it gained its 'Sir Berkeley' nameplates. It was moved to Byfield Quarry in 1959 but was finally withdrawn in 1963 after a lengthy period of storage. It entered preservation in 1964 when bought privately and loaned to the nascent Keighley & Worth Valley Railway. It was subsequently bought by the Vintage Carriages Trust and, as at 2015, is based at the Middleton Railway in Leeds, from where it makes visits to heritage lines both abroad and in the United Kingdom.

Right: **1210 is stabled as a display item in Barrow Hill Roundhouse on 12 April 2012 during a gala event dedicated to London North Eastern Railway operated locomotives.**

Opposite Page: **Making a 'guest' appearance on the Embsay & Bolton Abbey Railway, 1210 storms out of Bolton Abbey station on 6 October 2013 with a Bolton Abbey – Embsay service comprising a mix of vintage vehicles from various companies.**

Top Left: 0-4-0ST 1795 was supplied in 1912 to Thomas W Ward for duty at its Albion Works in Sheffield. It subsequently passed through many owners until arriving at Irchester Quarries in May 1957 from where it passed into preservation at the Quainton Railway Centre, subsequently the Buckinghamshire Railway Centre, on 27 August 1969 shortly after withdrawal. It has since been based at various locations with the latest being the Middleton Railway in Leeds from where 1795 is often loaned to other heritage locations mainly for display purposes. On 6 February 2014 it was on display at Barrow Hill Roundhouse, bearing the name 'E.B. Wilson' in tribute to the owner of the forerunner company of Manning Wardle.

Bottom Left: 0-6-0ST 1601 'Matthew Murray' was supplied in 1903 to P&W Anderson and Company for use in the construction of the Kent Portland Cement Works; following completion of the work the locomotive was sold to the cement company. It stayed there until withdrawal in 1967 then entered preservation with the Industrial Locomotive Preservation Company based on the Kent & East Sussex Railway. It was subsequently sold to the Middleton Railway where it arrived on 31 January 1990 and remains its current location as at 2016. On 28 May May 2004 it was noted as a display item at the National Rail Museum's York centre during the NRM's Railfest2004 gala event.

Bottom Right: 0-6-0ST 2047 'Warwickshire' was the last Manning Wardle locomotive to be built, being supplied to Rugby Cement Works in 1926. It was withdrawn from the New Bilton Works in 1966 and entered preservation with the Warwickshire Industrial Loco Preservation Group based on the Severn Valley Railway (SVR) where it remains as at 2016. On 24 September 2006 it was noted on static display at Kidderminster during the SVR's annual Autumn Steam Gala.

NBL: North British Locomotive Company

Date Established
1903

Location
Atlas Works; Hyde Park Works; Queens Park Works; All Glasgow

History
The firm was created by the merger of 3 local companies, each of which continued operating under the new company name. The 3 companies were Sharp Stewart and Company (Atlas Works); Neilson Reid and Company (Hyde Park Works) and Dubs and Company (Queens Park Works).

The company was adversely affected by the onset of BR's Dieselisation programme in the 1950s when it was restructured with financial support from the General Electric Company; Clydesdale Bank and HM Treasury to build diesel and electric locomotives. Its future, however, was badly affected by financial and quality problems made worse by the decision to sell its initial production to British Railways at a loss in order to regain the profit on future orders which were never realised. The firm entered voluntary liquidation on 19 April 1962.

0-6-0T 21521 was one of 3 locomotives built by NBL in 1917 for the Glasgow & South Western Railway (G&SWR) to the design of Peter Drummond as fleet number 7. The design was designated as the '5' Class but subsequently became '322' Class when 7 was renumbered to 324 in the G&SWR's 1919 renumbering scheme. The trio were subsequently renumbered 16377–9 when the G&SWR became part of the London Midland and Scottish Railway under the 1923 Grouping. 16378-9 were sold to Hatfield Colliery in 1934, and subsequently came into the ownership of the National Coal Board when it was created in 1948.

16379 was acquired by British Railways in 1963 and preserved in the Glasgow Museum of Transport until 2010 when it was moved to its current position, as at 2015, in the new Riverside Museum where it was photographed on 23 September 2014 replete in its original livery and G&SWR fleet number.

Date Established

1836

Location

Hyde Park Works, Springburn, Glasgow

History

The company began life as Nielson and Mitchell in 1836 but changed to Kerr Mitchell & Nielson following a move to new works in Hyde Park Street. It subsequently traded under a number of titles until 1845 when it became established as Neilson and Mitchell but then changed again in 1855 to become Neilson and Company when the company concentrated on railway locomotives.

In 1861 the company built a new works in Springburn, retaining the old site name, and in 1864 Henry Dubs left to create his own company whilst James Reid, a previous employee, returned as a partner. Neilson left the company in 1884 to found the Clyde Locomotive Company leaving James Reid as the sole owner; Reid only changed the company name to Neilson Reid and Company in 1898.

The company, along with Dubs and Company and Sharp Stewart and Company, amalgamated in 1903 to create the North British Locomotive Company [see **NBL=North British Locomotive Company**] as the largest locomotive company in the world outside the United States.

0-4-0ST 2203 was supplied to William Baird in 1876 to work at its Kelton Fell hematite mine in Cumberland where it was named 'Kelton Fell'. When the mine closed in 1914, 2203 was moved to Baird's Scottish coal mines, where it lost its name, and where it became owned by the National Coal Board in 1947. It finished its working life at Gartshore in March 1968 and entered preservation with the Scottish Railway Preservation Society (SRPS) at its Falkirk site. 2203 is now a permanent static exhibit at the SRPS Museum at Bo'ness where it was photographed on 17 August 2007.

Of interest is that the design proved so successful that Nielson & Co sold 4 locomotives to the Caledonian Railway which built a further 35 examples that survived to become 56001–38 in the British Railways fleet whilst it also sold 2 locomotives to the North British Railway Company which then built a further 36 examples that survived to become 68092–124 in the British Railways fleet.

NR: Nielson Reid & Company

See – Nn = Nielson & Company

0-6-2T 5408 was supplied to the Taff Vale Railway (TVR) in 1899, where it became fleet number 85, to work the coal trains between the Welsh Valleys and Cardiff Docks. When the TVR was absorbed by the Great Western Railway (GWR) in 1922, 5408 was made redundant by the GWR's policy of standardisation; withdrawn from service in 1927 it was sold to the Lambton, Hetton & Joicey Colliery in 1929 and subsequently passed to the National Coal Board in 1947.

As NCB No 52 it remained in service until 1968 then entered preservation at the Keighley & Worth Valley Railway (KWVR) in December 1970 where it was noted on 9 February 2003 working an Ingrow – Keighley Demonstration Freight train during the KWVR's Winter Steam Gala.

Date Established
1864

Location
Atlas Engine Works, Bristol

History
The company began as Fox Walker & Company, building 0-4-0 and 0-6-0 tank locomotives for industrial use, but was taken over in 1880 by Thomas Peckett who renamed the company to Thomas Peckett & Sons whilst continuing to build the same locomotives. The firm continued upto the 1950s; by 1950 trade had fallen off and, despite building some diesel mechanical locomotives, the last steam locomotive was built in 1958. The company was subsequently taken over by Reed Crane & Hoist Company on 23 October 1961 but that company also went into liquidation at a later date.

0-4-0ST 1163 was supplied to Cefnstylle Colliery Company in December 1908 for use at Gowerton Colliery and worked until 1922 when it was placed in store at the company's Berthlwyd Colliery. It remained there until 1936 when it was sold to Whitehead Hill & Co for use at its Oakfield Wire Works where it was named 'Whitehead' and continued working until becoming redundant at the end of 1966. It entered preservation in January 1967 with a private buyer based in Highbridge but the planned restoration didn't occur and 1163 was sold to the Great Western Society (Taunton Branch) in 1971 who initially moved it to Taunton then onto the West Somerset Railway in 1976. It was offered for sale in 1982 and bought by a Derbyshire couple who moved it to Southport's Steamport site where it remained until the Southport site closed in 1997. After being loaned to various heritage sites it finally moved to the Midland Railway Centre in July 1999 where it is based as at 2015 but from where it continues to visit other heritage sites.

Top: 1163 enters Barrow Hill Roundhouse on 12 July 2003 whilst working in top 'n tail mode with visiting engines on the shuttle service during a 'Tribute to the GWR' gala event.

Bottom Left: 0-4-0ST 1370 'May' was supplied to Yates Duxbury & Sons for use in their paper mill at Heaps Bridge on the outskirts of Bury where it worked until 1970. It entered preservation with the Beet family collection based at Carnforth before transferring to the East Lancashire Railway from where it visits other sites including the Ribble Steam Railway where it was noted on 2 April 2011 working a Riversway – Strand Road shuttle service.

Top Right: 0-4-0ST 1370 was also used by the Ribble Steam Railway as a static exhibit for a short period as noted on 23 February 2011 when it was positioned inside the museum building.

Bottom Right: 0-4-0ST 1690 was supplied in 1926 to Gypsum Mines Ltd to work at its Kingston upon Soar site where it was named 'Lady Angela'. It worked there until the 1970s when it entered preservation at the Shackerstone Railway but was subsequently bought by Dennis Braybrook and moved to the Dart Valley Railway (DVR) in July 1976. Following Dennis's death, his widow gifted 1690 to the DVR where it was seen as a display item at Buckfastleigh on 22 June 2012.

Bottom Left: 0-4-0ST 1636 was supplied in 1924 to the Aberthaw & Bristol Channel Portland Cement Company for work at its Aberthaw site and subsequently at the Tumen Asbestos Works in nearby Rhoose. It entered preservation at the Bitton Railway Centre (later Avon Valley Railway) in September 1974 where it worked until expiry of its boiler certificate in 1990, leading to a sale to the Spa Valley Railway where it was photographed awaiting overhaul on 17 June 2011.

OPPOSITE PAGE

Left: 0-4-0ST 1803 was supplied in 1933 to Ironbridge Power Station where it worked until the 1970s. On withdrawal it was bought privately and entered preservation at the Foxfield Steam Railway (FSR) on 19 September 1980. It was restored to working order but as at 2015 it is 'out of ticket' and is now on display at the FSR's Caverswall Road Museum awaiting overhaul and where it was photographed on 7 April 2013.

Right: 0-4-0ST 1722 was supplied to Courtaulds in 1926 to work at its Coventry site where it worked until withdrawal in 1972. It then became part of the 'Shropshire Collection' and moved to a site near Shrewsbury until 2003 when it was moved to the Telford Steam Railway (TSR). The TSR subsequently bought the locomotive and it remains one of its main operating locomotives as on 28 May 2006 when it was active on one of the TSR's shuttle services.

CURRENT PAGE

Top: 1722 sits in Telford yard after completing its day of working shuttle services around the site.

Bottom: 0-4-0ST 1749 'Fulstow' was supplied in 1928 to Cawdor Quarry, Matlock where it remained throughout its working life until withdrawal in 1970. It entered preservation with a private buyer and, as at 2016, is based at the Lincolnshire Wolds Railway from where it makes occasional visits to other heritage lines. In 2011 it visited the Ribble Steam Railway where, on 17 September 17 2015, it was noted working a Strand Road – Riversway shuttle service in tandem with resident Andrew Barclay 0-4-0ST 1147 'John Howe'.

0-6-0ST 2000 was supplied to the British Sugar Corporation (BSC) in 1942 for use at its Colwick factory; it remained until 1955 then, after overhaul by Pecketts, was moved to the BSC's Ipswich factory from where it was withdrawn in 1977. It then entered preservation at the Nene Valley Railway but subsequently moved to the Barrow Hill Roundhouse where, as at 2016, it is now based.

2000 enters Barrow Hill Roundhouse yard on 21 October 2006 whilst working in top 'n tail mode with 'Manor' Class 4-6-0 7822 'Foxcote Manor' on a shuttle service during a gala event.

Left: 2000 starts the shuttle service on its return journey, in top 'n tail mode with 'V2' Class 2-6-2 4771 Green Arrow, to the Barrow Hill platform on 10 november 2007.

Top: 2000 drifts towards the Barrow Hill Roundhouse entrance on 23 August 2008 whilst working a shuttle service in top 'n tail mode with L&Y 3F 0-6-0 1300.

Bottom: 2000 receives the signal to enter Barrow Hill on 10 November 2007 whilst drawing the shuttle service back to the platform when working in top 'n tail mode with an unidentified locomotive.

0-4-0ST 2081 was supplied to the City of Birmingham Gas Department in 1947 to work at Nechells Gas Works, where the tight curves called for a modified OY design. It was transferred to Swan Village Gas Works in 1965 and on withdrawal in 1969 entered preservation at the Foxfield Steam Railway where it arrived on 17 August 1969.

0-4-0ST 2084 was supplied to Courtaulds in 1948 to work at its site in Flint, North Wales. When replaced by diesels it entered preservation with the Llangollen Railway from where it was sold to a scrap merchant at Mold; it was bought on 23 July 1986 and moved to the West Coast Railway Company base at Carnforth for restoration. When completed 2084 was moved to the Kirkby Stephen East site of the nascent Stainmore Railway where it was named 'F.C. Tingey' in honour of a volunteer who died before seeing it steam.

Top: 2084 provides a display item at the SR's Kirkby Stephen East on 3 June 2006 in the early days of the Stainmore Railway.

Bottom: 2084 is prepared for action on 27 August 2011 during the SR's 150th Anniversary celebration at Kirkby Stephen East.

OPPOSITE PAGE

Left: 2081 is on display at the FSR's Caverswall Road museum on 7 April 2013 whilst awaiting overhaul.

Top Right: 2081 is on display in Caverswall Road shed yard on 9 August 2014 during a gala event.

Bottom Right: 0-4-0ST 2004 was supplied to the General Electric Company (GEC) in 1941 to work at its Swinton site. When withdrawn from service it entered preservation at the Birmingham Railway Museum (later Tyseley Locomotive Works) where it is still based as at 2016. It occasionally appears as 6 'Percy' (from the Thomas the Tank' stories) but on the Open Day held on 24 June 2012 it appeared in its usual red lined livery to work the Demonstration Freight train.

RSH: Robert Stephenson & Hawthorn

Date Established
1937

Location
Darlington; Newcastle on Tyne

History
The company was formed in 1937 by the amalgamation of Robert Stephenson & Co of Darlington and Hawthorn Leslie & Co of Newcastle [see **HL=Hawthorn Leslie & Company**] leading to the new company taking the name of Robert Stephenson & Hawthorn from September 1937; the new company later took over the assets and goodwill of Kitson & Company in 1938 [see **K=Kitson & Co**].

The new company sought to continue production of industrial locomotives at its Newcastle site and main line locomotives at its Darlington site although on occasion locomotives were built at the most convenient site for particular orders. At the date of amalgamation the latest works number issued by Hawthorn Leslie & Company was 2783 and that by Robert Stephenson & Company 4155; these were combined to give 6938 hence the first works number issued by the new concern was 6939.

The company was an early builder of diesel locomotives and during the 1950s steam locomotive production declined as the company adapted to the new order and, in 1955 became part of the English Electric group. Benefitting from the British Railways Modernisation Plan, the company built batches of Classes 04; 20; 37 and 40 before the orders ceased, leading to the closure of the Newcastle site in 1961 and the Darlington site in 1964.

0-4-0CT 7006 'Roker' was supplied to William Doxford & Sons in 1940 to their shipbuilding yard in Sunderland and followed the design of an earlier locomotive supplied by Hawthorn Leslie in 1902. 7006 and its ilk were replaced by road cranes in 1971 with 7006 being sold for scrap; it was bought privately but sold on to the Foxfield Steam Railway (FSR) where it arrived in July 1974 and where it is still based as at 2016. On a visit to the FSR's Caverswall Road Museum on 7 April 2013, 7006 was a display item whilst awaiting overhaul to working condition.

Bottom: 0-4-0CT 7069 'Southwick' was supplied to William Doxford & Sons in 1942 to the same design as 7006 and when replaced by road cranes it entered preservation at the Keighley & Worth Valley Railway where it was noted on 10 February 2012 stored in the siding at Ingrow awaiting an overhaul to working condition.

Top: 0-4-0ST 7063 was supplied to Dunston B Power Station (Gateshead) in 1942 where it was named 'Eustace Forth'. It worked until 1972 then entered preservation when bought by the Hexham Rolling Stock Group and moved to the North Yorkshire Moors Railway. 7063 was subsequently placed on loan with the National Rail Museum which exhibits it at both York and Shildon; on 13 September 2011 it was on display at Shildon.

0-6-0T 7765 was supplied to the National Coal Board in 1954 for work at Ashington Colliery and worked until 1969 when it was replaced by the influx of redundant British Railways Class 14 diesel locomotives. 7765 entered preservation at the Colne Valley Railway shortly after but was bought by the Weardale Railway (WR), returning north to the WR on 3 November 2006, where it is based as at 2016.

On 13 September 2011 7765 was powering services on the WR and scenes at Stanhope noted 7765 *Right:* departing with a service to Wolsingham and *Bottom:* preparing to couple up to a service for Wolsingham.

0-6-0ST 7485 was one of 3 similar locomotives supplied to the Salford Corporation Electricity Department in 1948 to work at its Agecroft Power Station, between Manchester and Bolton, where it was named 'Agecroft No 2'. When the engines were replaced by a conveyor belt operating directly between colliery and power station, they were offered for sale and 7485 entered preservation on 14 December 1982 at Southport Steamport Museum.

7485 remained as a Steamport locomotive and when the operation moved to Preston to create the Ribble Steam Railway (RSR), it moved and continued to work at the new site. Whilst the RSR site was being created, 7485 was loaned to the East Lancashire Railway during 2004 where it masqueraded as 6 'Percy' from the 'Thomas the Tank' series. It was withdrawn from service with the RSR in November 2008 and, as at 2015, still awaits its place in the overhaul queue.

Top Left: 7485 performed the official Opening Ceremony of the RSR on 17 September 2005 and poses at Riversway platform before breaking through the barrier with the first shuttle service to Strand Road headshunt.

Bottom Left: The RSR held an Open Day on 8 January 2005 to display its progress in preparation for the official opening in September 2005 and 7485 is seen arriving with a shuttle service run in conjunction with the event.

Bottom Right: 7485 crosses the Marina Bridge on 26 June 2005 with a Riversway–Strand Road shuttle service.

Whilst the RSR was being established, it was required to operate a regular train service to test the condition of the line between Strand Road and the new development. The train was worked in top 'n tail mode and on 13 July 2003 it was 7485 (with Sentinel 10282 'Enterprise' on the rear) which led the train as it approached the Marina Bridge with the return working.

Top Left: 7485 emerges onto the Marina Bridge roadway with a Riversway–Strand Road shuttle on 17 September 2005. *Top Right:* 7485 crosses the Marina Bridge on 17 September 2005 with a Riversway–Strand Road shuttle service. *Bottom Left:* 7485 provides the rear end of a Riversway–Strand Road shuttle service on 18 May 2008, powered by Sentinel 0-4-0VB 8024 'Gasbag'. *Bottom Right:* Following withdrawal from service 7485 provides a museum exhibit on 23 February 2011 whilst awaiting overhaul.

0-6-0ST 7086 was an 'Austerity' locomotive built to the Hunslet Engine Company's Class 50555 deign and supplied to the Ministry of Supply in 1943 as WD 75050, being delivered to Long Marston on 24 April 1943. After seeing war service in Europe it was sold to Doncaster Amalgamated Colliery Ltd where it worked until moved to Askern Main Colliery in 1970 where it was kept as 'spare' engine. It was sold to the Titanic Steamship Company in 1976 and entered preservation at the Kent & East Sussex Railway in 1979 where it became fleet number 27 named 'Rolvenden'. It was subsequently bought by Southern Locomotives Ltd and overhauled for use on the Swanage Railway but is also available for hire to heritage lines. As at 2016 7086 is on long-term hire to the Embsay & Bolton Abbey Railway (EBAR).

Digital photography allows images to be changed dramatically and quickly as this pair of images shows. 7086 'Norman' was photographed climbing through Draughton on the EBAR with a Demonstration Freight Train on 4 May 2013 during a Gala event. *Right:* **is the original photograph taken in portrait format whilst** *Bottom:* **shows the same scene after the image has been cropped to landscape format.**

An earlier incarnation of 68005 was that of 0-6-0ST 7169 which was supplied to the Ministry of Supply in 1944 as WD 71515 but sold in 1946 to the Mechanical Navvies Ltd for use at Swalwell Disposal Point in County Durham. It entered preservation at the East Somerset Railway in 1974 where it was repainted to represent British Railways Class J94 0-6-0ST 68005. It was hired to the Embsay & Bolton Abbey Railway in 1995 and overhauled in 2004 but a burst boiler tube saw it stored in 2006. In August 2009 a member of the Pontypool & Blaenavon Railway (P&BR) bought 7169 and had it moved to the Flour Mill in the Forest of Dean for repair and repaint into its Mechanical Navvies livery and branding prior to moving it to the P&BR where it is permanently based as at 2016.

Top: During 2013 7086 was repainted to represent British Railways Class J94 0-6-0ST 68005, in which guise it was noted stabled between duties at Bolton Abbey on 6 October 2013 during a Branch Line gala event.

Bottom: 7169, in the guise of British Railways Class J94 0-6-0ST 68005, stands at Bolton Abbey on 15 October 2005 awaiting departure with a service for Embsay during a gala event.

At the end of WWII, the firm of Stewarts & Lloyds (S&L) sought to expand its network of quarry lines around the Corby area and the company wanted a locomotive more powerful than its current fleet of locomotives, built to the same 16″ design by Manning Wardle then Kitsons and finally Robert Stephenson & Hawthorn (RSH) as successors in title. The Minerals Department borrowed Hunslet Engine Company 0-6-0ST 2411 from the Steelworks Department for a 2-week trial period, as a result of which a design specification was prepared for RSH to build.

S&L ordered 7 locomotives (RSH 7667–7673 allocated S&L fleet numbers 56–62) followed by further orders for RSH 7761/S&L 63 in 1954 and RSH 8050/S&L 64 in 1958. These 9 locomotives were replaced by Class 14 diesel locomotives when sold by British Railways in 1968 and, following a period in store, RSH 7668 (S&L57); RSH 7673 (S&L 62) and RSH 7761 (S&L 63) entered preservation at the Keighley & Worth Valley Railway (KWVR) in May 1969 whilst RSH 7667 (S&L 56) was bought by a private buyer.

In preservation the locomotives gained the epithet of 'Uglies' but their power made them useful; as the KWVR became established it needed more powerful locomotives and by the 1980s its 'Uglies' were placed in store and subsequently sold to other heritage lines. As at 2016 RSH 7667 / S&L 56 and RSH 7761 / S&L 63 are based at the Great Central Railway (North) located at Ruddington by Nottingham whilst RSH 7668 / S&L 57 and RSH 7673 / S&L 62 are based on the Spa Valley Railway.

In July 2012 7673 / S&L 62 was the 'guest' locomotive at the Foxfield Steam Railway's Summer Gala and a visit was made to the event on 21 July when 7673 was 'chartered' by photographers to work in Foxfield Colliery before the programmed event timetable began. 7673 was noted drifting down Foxfield Bank en route to the colliery and the start of the charter session.

Scenes from the charter include:

Left/Bottom: 7673 ascending Foxfield Bank on the gradient out of the colliery and *Top:* setting up a train in the colliery yard.

7673 climbs out of Foxfield Colliery on the ascent of Foxfield Bank during a photographer's charter on 21 July 2012.

S: Sentinel

Date Established
1915

Location
Sentinel Works, Shrewsbury

History
The company originated in Glasgow in 1875 as Alley & MacLellan to manufacture valves and compressors for steam engines but in 1903 it acquired Simpson & Bibby of Horsehay which manufactured steam powered road vehicles. In 1915 Alley & MacLellan established a new factory at Shrewsbury to manufacture steam powered vehicles which traded as Sentinel Waggon Works Ltd. Their product line included steam locomotives which continued after the company was bought by William Beardmore & Company in 1917 but the bulk of production was of road vehicles. In 1946 Sentinel agreed with Thomas Hill to act as agent for the repair and maintenance of diesel engines by a contract which was extended in 1947 to cover steam locomotives.

By the 1950s steam locomotive production was on the wane and the company was acquired by Rolls-Royce in 1956 to produce diesel engines whilst in 1963 Thomas Hill decided to renew its locomotive agreements but restricting them to the maintenance of steam locomotives only. The last steam locomotives built were in 1958 for Dorman Long but that company turned to diesel traction after the order was placed and so never took delivery of them; the pair were subsequently converted to diesel hydraulic locomotives.

Top: 0-4-0VBT 9373 'St Monans' was supplied to Hawton Plaster Works (later British Gypsum) in 1947 to work at its Newark site. It was replaced by a diesel locomotive and entered preservation at the Great Central Railway at Loughborough from where it was re-sold and moved to Southport Steamport Museum in 1979. Its working life was halted by a failed superheater in the early 1990s but it was moved to the Ribble Steam Railway site at Preston on 13 March 1999 where it is now a static exhibit. On 27 October 2014 9373 was stored in the recently built Furness Trust shed building awaiting a move to the Museum display area.

Bottom: 0-4-0VBT 8024 was supplied to the Gas Board in Cambridge in 1929 to work and on withdrawal entered preservation at Carnforth Steamtown. It fell into disuse and was purchased in 1997 and transferred to Southport Steamport Museum and consequently to the Ribble Steam Railway site at Preston on 23 March 1999. It was used in tandem with Andrew Barclay 0-4-0ST 1147 'John Howe' on 18 May 2008 working a Riversway–Strand Road shuttle but, as at 2016, 8024 awaits overhaul hence its appearance in the RSR Museum as a static exhibit.

VF: Vulcan Foundry

Date Established

1830

Location

Vulcan Works, Newton le Willows

History

The site was initially opened as Charles Tayleur & Company but in 1832 Robert Stephenson selected the company to build locomotives to reduce the distance between the adjacent Liverpool & Manchester Railway and his original site at Newcastle on Tyne. From 1847 the company traded as The Vulcan Foundry Company upto 1898 when 'the' was dropped. Steam locomotive construction continued until 1956, the company having become part of the English Electric group in 1955, and the works concentrated on the construction of both diesel and electric locomotives. The company passed through further ownership changes but in 2002 the works closed and the site was levelled in 2007 to become a housing estate of 630 houses that was started in 2010.

0-4-0ST 3272 was built in 1918 and was retained by the company as its yard shunter. Its entry into preservation is uncertain but after time spent at Peak Rail it moved to Barrow Hill Roundhouse where it is based as at 2016. It has also been loaned from there, visiting both Beamish and the Ribble Steam Railway as 'guest' locomotive for gala events.

Digital photography allows images to be changed dramatically and quickly as this pair of images shows. 3272 was photographed at Barrow Hill on 6 February 2014 during a Gala event when it powered a Demonstration Freight Train on the branch line as part of a photography charter. *Right:* is an image concentrating on the train whilst *Opposite:* is the original photograph from which the previous image was taken.

Top: 3272 enters Barrow Hill yard on 6 February 2014 with a Demonstration Freight train during a photo charter session.

Bottom: 3272 provides the rear of a shuttle service in Barrow Hill yard on 29 September 2013 during a gala event.

WCI: Wigan Coal & Iron Company

Date Established
1865

Location
Kirkless Workshops, Wigan

History
In the 19th century many collieries in the Wigan area built their own locomotives and in 1865 these amalgamated to form the Wigan Coal & Iron Company with locomotives being built at the main workshops at Kirkless. The company continued operating through the 19th century and even had locomotives built by other contractors to their designs – including Nasmyth Wilson who built 4 locomotives between 1892–1902. There is little information about this company and it seems to have ceased building locomotives around 1912.

0-6-0ST 'Lindsay' was built in 1887 for service in the local collieries where it remained until the creation of the National Coal Board in 1947 and continued working until the 1960s. Its final location was at Hafod Colliery by Wrexham from where it was sent to Maudlands Metals scrapyard in Preston for disposal. It was rescued from there in 1976 by the Lindsay Loco Trust which restored it then moved it to Carnforth Steamtown in 1981 and where the locomotive is still based as at 2016. The locomotive is not available to public view but the site held an Open Day on 26 July 2008 when it was one of the display items.

YE: Yorkshire Engine Company

Date Established

1865

Location

Meadowhall Works, Sheffield

History

The company was formed in 1865 and concentrated on small industrial locomotives for collieries and quarries. It remained an independent company throughout its life, building steam locomotives between 1865–1956 and diesel locomotives between 1950–1965. The firm was bought by the United Steel Company in June 1945 as this latter company was looking to both build its own locomotives to service its steelworks and establish a central maintenance centre for its local steelworks at Rotherham and Stocksbridge. This continued until the threat of steel nationalisation in the 1960s when YE was sold to Rolls Royce in 1965 and work was transferred to its Shrewsbury site [see **S = Sentinel**] leading to closure of the Sheffield site which subsequently became the access point of the South Yorkshire Locomotive Preservation Society whose site was adjacent to the Meadowhall Works.

0-6-0ST 2521 was built to the Hunslet 48150 design and supplied in 1952 to the Appleby-Frodingham steelworks at Scunthorpe where it worked until displaced by diesel locomotives in the 1960s. It was sold to the National Coal Board for use at Clipstone Colliery before passing to the National Coal Mining Museum. It has since been loaned to various sites but at 2016 is based at the Barrow Hill Roundhouse where work to restore it to working order has fallen off. On 28 August 2008, 2521 was stabled inside the Roundhouse awaiting decisions as to its future.